If You're Hurting...

I've written this book to be an encouragement to all those who are walking through a difficult time in their lives. The cause could be an illness (as was my case—I had cancer), the loss of a loved one, a divorce, financial difficulties, or any number of situations that cause sorrow. These prayers and meditations are for anyone who finds herself wandering through the valley of darkness. When my life looks down, I've learned to look upward. May these spiritual inspirations help ease your pain. May God's wisdom set your feet on solid ground and give you hope for tomorrow.

Emilie

God Preserves Your Tears

The psalmist David was amazed that God was attentive to every detail of his life—even down to the tears he shed. It truly is amazing to think that our God is so intimately concerned for us that He notices our tears and saves them in His bottle. During my journey with illness and trials, I have shed many tears—some of joy and some of pain. Even minor tears are huge to the one who cries. God uses these times to cleanse us. Don't be afraid to cry—it's a release for the soul. God says that He preserves each and every one of our tears.

You have seen me tossing and turning through the night. You have collected all my tears and preserved them in your bottle! You have recorded every one in your book.

PSALM 56:8

4

When pain comes into our lives, we are tempted to ask "Why, Lord?" Everyone has experienced some kind of tragedy. If not yet, it will come. How we handle these events when they happen is key. Whatever your test today is, please know that others have experienced similar pain. Don't go through it alone. Contact your local church or hospital or support group to find out what programs are offered.

Jesus has also experienced our pain. When I think of the pain He suffered on the cross for me, my load seems much lighter. This has given me more courage to fight my battle. He is always with us to help us get through the tough times of life. Trust Him now.

Trust Him

Trust in the LORD with all your heart and lean not on your own understanding.

PROVERBS 3:5 NIV

5

No Busy Signals

I want men everywhere

to pray. . .

1 TIMOTHY 2:8

Prayer is honored by our Lord, and we are commanded and told to have personal communion with Him. It is not something we have to do, but something we get to do. What a privilege! We need not make an appointment to get His attention. He is always available: "The Lord is near to all who call upon Him" (Psalm 145:18 NIV). We aren't screened by an answering machine, caller ID, an administrative assistant, or a group of secretaries. Nope. God is always there for us. He never is too busy. He will never say, "Call back when My calendar isn't so full." We are invited to walk boldly into His presence at any moment, day or night.

Not Yet!

Weeping may go on all night, but in the morning there is joy.

PSALM 30:5

God does not afflict or grieve the children of man for nothing. He shows this by the fact that He never allows affliction to last longer than there is a need for. Do not be discouraged when you suffer. He shall make your vineyard blossom and your field to yield its fruit. You shall again come forth with those who rejoice, and once more shall the song of gladness be on your lips. Hope yet, for there is hope. He shall bring you up from the land of your captivity, and you shall say of Him, "Thou hast turned for me my mourning into dancing" (Psalm 30:11 KJV).

Lord, for whatever I am receiving and about to receive—pain as well as joy—please teach me the secret of giving thanks for what I have already received, what has shaped my life in the past, and what is shaping me today. Please do not let my yesterdays spoil today. Please fill my life with thanksgiving. Let me reach out and encourage others who are in similar circumstances with the same comfort that You have bestowed on me. Amen.

Do you ever catch your thoughts taking a negative turn? Most of us are very good at finding the problems in our situations. I suggest that you develop a more positive thought process. When I know that God is thinking about me constantly, how can I not think positive of myself and my situation? We aren't being conceited when we recognize the good in our life—however, we must recognize that all good comes from our heavenly Father.

Many times, after going through a delicate medical procedure, my Bob and I would celebrate by doing something special as recognition that I had done a "good job." Keep telling yourself the positive—don't let the negative take hold of your thought process.

God Is Thinking of You

How precious it is, Lord, to realize that you are thinking about me constantly! I can't even count how many times a day your thoughts turn toward me.

PSALM 139:17

9

You Will Smile Again

There were times when I didn't think I would smile or laugh again. This verse helped me to remember, "He will make me smile again." Don't you just love that? When my spirit becomes gloomy, I choose to continually trust in God. Despite what's happening in our lives, we can say, "We will not fear!" God has given me confidence that I can believe Him for the future. He is our refuge and strength.

It feels so good to smile. It's one of the most therapeutic exercises we can do. A smile reflects the confidence we have in our Lord. We trust Him enough to reflect a sign of joy—a big bright smile.

Oh my soul, why be so gloomy and discouraged? Trust in God! I shall again praise him for his wondrous help; he will make me smile again, for he is my God!

PSALM 43:5

Words That Encourage

Never in my life have I enjoyed reading God's Word as much as in the past years of trials. Taking in the sweet words, verse after verse, has brought me such encouragement. As I read and meditate on these precious words, my soul is refreshed with a new sense of God's promises and faithfulness. Even familiar passages take on new meaning, and I enjoy them like never before.

Revisiting Scriptures that have had meaning at different points in my life serves to remind me of God's presence throughout the trials and joys of a lifetime. This security offers me assurance that God will be with me every step of the way.

For everything that was written in the past was written to teach us, so that through endurance and the encouragement of the Scriptures we might have hope.

ROMANS 15:4 NIV

From Worry to Prayer

Pastor Chuck Swindoll says there are six words that should clearly be fixed in our minds. These six words form the foundation of God's therapeutic process for all worry-warts: Worry about nothing. Pray about everything.

Worry is one of the great negatives for the mind. We waste so much time worrying! It literally drains all of the joy from our presence.

I have found that I need to take items from my "worry list" and put them on my "prayer list." Now *that's* a list we can do something about. Transfer your anxieties from worry to prayer. That way you can be proactive about your situation and rest in His perfect will.

The Right Perspective

You are my refuge and my shield, and your promises are my only source of hope.

PSALM 119:114

How can I be so upbeat when so many things around me are negative? It's because of my perspective on life. Through Scripture and life experiences, I have come to trust that God has a plan for my life. I can count on His promises. When the psalmist tells me that God is my shield and that His promises are my only source of hope, I believe it. God's Word brings me light on a foggy day and hope when I become discouraged. It helps me not to make a mountain out of a molehill. His Word gives me the right perspective on life. I know my time on earth is such a short time and my time with Him after this earthly experience will be for eternity.

Live Each Day

Teach us to number our days and
recognize how few they are; help us
to spend them as we should.

PSALM 90:12

How often do we talk in terms of days? Usually our reference is in terms of years. This verse suggests that we are to number our days. We're encouraged to live each day to the fullest so that when our life draws to an end, we've spent each day as we should—with gusto and enthusiasm for the Lord.

I've found that as I go through trials I must learn to adjust to the unknowns that appear. One can only do this from day to day and often from hour to hour. It doesn't do any good to become negative. Rather, celebrate the life that God has given you...today.

Father God, I want to open my heart and learn from the trials I have. However, I struggle at times. My natural self wants to resist these trials. Thank You for understanding my humanness. Amen.

When You Are Angry...

If you are angry, don't sin by nursing your grudge. Don't let the sun go down with you still angry—get over it quickly; for when you are angry you give a mighty foothold to the devil.

EPHESIANS 4:26-27

Oh yes, there were times when I was angry at God. Yet through all the testings of my faith, I came to a better understanding of life. And even though I was angry, I never gave up on God, and I never lost trust in Him as my strength and my shield. God didn't get smaller. In fact, He became bigger than ever.

Satan was not going to gain victory over me during my suffering. I knew that God didn't give me cancer. But since the germs of the fallen world permitted my body to contract this disease, I was going to make the best of it—and God was going to gain the glory.

16

God may heal directly, through medicine, or in answer to prayer. When I was first diagnosed with cancer, I went to the elders of the church and asked them to pray for me and anoint me with oil. It was a beautiful ceremony. I had never been anointed with oil before, thus I didn't know what to expect. However, I was desiring complete healing. When I wasn't immediately healed I felt disappointed and was let down temporarily—not wanting to accept the fact that God said, "Not yet." It wasn't until many months later that I could see and feel the effects of my healing taking place.

A Prayer Offered in Faith

Is anyone sick? He should call for the elders of the church and they should pray over him and pour a little oil upon him, calling on the Lord to heal him.

JAMES 5:14

17

More Than We Ask For

Now to Him who is able to do exceeding abundantly beyond all that we ask or think, according to the power that works within us, to Him be the glory...

EPHESIANS 3:20-21 NIV

In my recent journey of despair, I had reached the end of the road (so I thought). There was one ray of hope available for my illness—a bone-marrow transplant. We tried to match with my brother, our son, and our daughter; none worked. We sent out an S.O.S. for a donor and back came a perfect match from a 23-year-old Canadian male. He didn't know me, and I didn't know him, but God knew us both. I was accepted by the Fred Hutchinson Cancer Research Center in Seattle, Washington, to be a nonrelated bone-marrow recipient. I was blessed by God to successfully receive healthy bone marrow from this young man. God truly gave me more than we could have ever expected. He can do the same in your situation.

Sometimes we stroll along life's busy highways with good health, humming a song, without a trouble in the world. Suddenly a trial raises its ugly head, and we come to a screeching halt. *Help!* What do we do? We begin to pray. "Lord, for whatever we receive now and what we will receive in the future—pain as well as joy—please teach us the secret of giving thanks. May we reach out and encourage other lives that are in similar circumstances with the same comfort that You have bestowed on us."

Jesus is the ultimate comforter. It is only when we go to Him that we will find the healing and hope we desire.

The Comforter

What a wonderful God we have—he is the Father of our Lord Jesus Christ, the source of every mercy, and the one who so wonderfully comforts and strengthens us in our hardships and trials.

2 CORINTHIANS 1:3-4

Father God, little or big, I bring my needs before You. If
You number the sands on the beach, You are surely interested
in the details of my life. Thank You for majoring on the
minors of life. You are an awesome God. Amen.

God truly wants us to pray about the simple and small things of life. He is a God of the household as well as the God of the heavens. We should be specific in identifying all that we want to mention before God. We can pray for anything! God is concerned about even the smallest of our desires. Visualize that God is instantly in the process of answering your "household" requests, and watch Him work great things during your time of suffering.

God Is in the Small Stuff

In everything by prayer and supplication with thanksgiving let your requests be made known to God.

PHILIPPIANS 4:6 KJV

You Are My Hiding Place

Thou art my hiding place

and my shield...

PSALM 119:114 KJV

As a little girl, I loved to play hide-and-seek. When it started to get dark, I delighted to find a secret place where no one could find me. I felt secure knowing that no one was going to catch me. When I became a Christian and started to have a daily quiet time with my Lord, I was soon aware that my "prayer closet" had become my new hiding place. This was a place where I felt safe from the world, and I could take all the time I needed to read God's Word.

When you feel the stress of the day getting to you, think of the safety you feel in your hiding place—Jesus. Knowing God is always with you will calm your spirit.

Let Jesus' light and your present situation lead you to truth that will put you in the presence of God. I have met countless people who have found Jesus through their journey of pain or loss. Even though I came into my own difficulties as a believer, I have experienced an abundance of growth in my Christian walk during this time. As my focus turned off myself and onto God, I was able to sing praises to His name. This grander view of what is important opened my eyes to God's goodness in the midst of even my greatest needs.

Light and Truth

Oh, send out your light and your truth—let them lead me.

PSALM 43:3

No More Suffering

These troubles and sufferings of ours are, after all, quite small and won't last very long. Yet this short time of distress will result in God's richest blessing upon us forever and ever!

2 CORINTHIANS 4:17

Sometimes my affliction seems so big and I have endured so long that I become discouraged. I can hardly believe this illness is actually happening to me. I want to be well and go back to my normal way of life. Then, the Holy Spirit reassures me not to lose hope, not to be discouraged. Even though my outer self is decaying, this affliction is light and temporary when set against eternity.

The Scriptures tell me that by enduring these earthly troubles I will inherit blessings for eternity. I know I look forward to a time and place with no more pain and suffering.

On our patio, we have a wonderful three-tiered fountain that echoes the splashing of water as it falls from one tier to another. The sound of the water is so tranquil. I love to sit and listen to its soothing sounds. I feel rejuvenated in a short time. Quite often I reflect on all the delights God has bestowed on my life. He has given me more than I would have ever thought possible. Even if my quality of life doesn't get any better, I will praise the Lord for being so good to me. At times, I thought I'd never be back to this level of recovery.

The Father's light has certainly illuminated my path. I no longer need to walk in darkness.

Fountain of Life

You give them drink from your river of delights. For with you is the fountain of life; in your light we see light.

PSALM 36:8-9 NIV

Father God, even in my peril You tell me "not yet." When I beg for relief You utter "not yet." I know all these sufferings are molding me into the person You want me to become. Help me keep my eyes on You for my deliverance. Amen.

Have you ever felt like quitting? I know I have. I'm not very competitive, so *hanging in there* is not always in my vocabulary. My son, who is a triathlete and runs marathons, would tell me in a small voice, "Mom, no pain, no gain." Just what I didn't want to hear.

Hang in there—don't let the enemy defeat you. I know there are many days when you want to run and hide, but believe me, there is light at the end of the tunnel. When you first see that light, you will be so glad that you didn't quit.

No Pain, No Gain

Happy is the man who doesn't give in and do wrong when he is tempted, for afterwards he will get as his reward the crown of life that God has promised those who love him.

JAMES 1:12

Restore the Joy

Joy always follows sorrow. I've met so many people who are right in the middle of sorrow—a death, a divorce, a serious health problem, teenage children that are rebelling, financial difficulties, an unbelieving mate. The list goes on and on.

Each of us, at one time or another, has been in deep sorrow. Sometimes it seems as if we will never smile again because the burden is so heavy and the load is so great. Yet in our deepest sorrow, we can plead to God, "Restore to me again the joy of your salvation" (Psalm 51:12). The load then becomes lighter, and we can pray to God to continue our joy even during our deepest times of trouble.

28

Take Great and Little Things to Him

Let the little children come to me, and don't prevent them.

MATTHEW 19:14

God, our Father, is a good father. He is powerful enough to count the stars and calls them by name, yet He also hears and heals the brokenhearted and binds up their wounds. If you have put your confidence in God, you can take great concerns and little concerns to Him, knowing He will never disappoint your faith. He has said that those who trust Him will "never be disappointed in their God through all eternity" (Isaiah 45:17).

God always hears the prayers of the ones who love Him.

29

Expect the Troubles

I have learned the secret of

contentment in every situation...

for I can do everything God asks

me to with the help of Christ who

gives me the strength and power.

PHILIPPIANS 4:12-13

Why are so many people surprised when life is difficult? Jesus told us life would be difficult and troublesome. However, so many think they're entitled to a trouble-free life—nothing but happiness, fun, and financial success.

Then, when trouble inevitably comes, they're devastated. I have learned to expect the problems and let them teach me something...such as what's really important in life.

Best of all, I'm learning it's possible to feel content and peaceful even while bad things are happening—because I know it's all temporary. I can expect pain and trouble because that's part of living in the world, but I can trust God's promise that He'll carry me through it all.

A famous old violin maker always made his instruments out of wood from the north side of the tree. Why? Because the wood which had endured the brunt of the fierce wind, icy snow, and raging storm lent a finer tone to the violin. Trouble and sorrow give the soul its sweetest melodies.

One whose security is in God can be steadfast and unmovable at all times and in any situation. When life seems to crash upon you, you can say, "My soul is bowed down, but my heart is fixed." When we have this security and stability, we can sing a precious song of victory.

Yes, God knows our situation. It's easy to sing when the days are bright, but a steadfast heart can also sing in times of trouble.

Sing Confident Praises

O God, my heart is quiet
and confident. No wonder
I can sing your praises!

PSALM 57:7

31

Reaping Joy

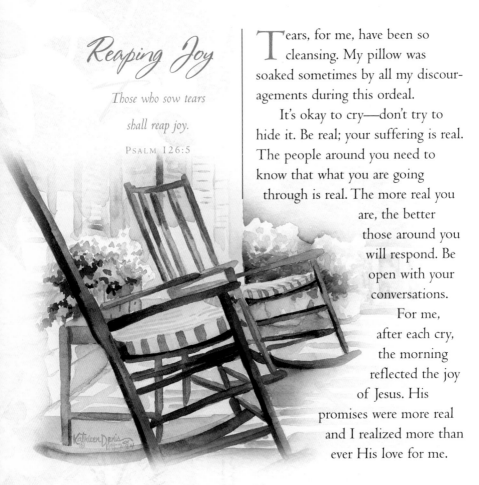

Those who sow tears

shall reap joy.

PSALM 126:5

Tears, for me, have been so cleansing. My pillow was soaked sometimes by all my discouragements during this ordeal.

It's okay to cry—don't try to hide it. Be real; your suffering is real. The people around you need to know that what you are going through is real. The more real you are, the better those around you will respond. Be open with your conversations.

For me, after each cry, the morning reflected the joy of Jesus. His promises were more real and I realized more than ever His love for me.

32

The apostle Paul, who suffered much during his lifetime, realized that though our material possessions can be wonderful and enjoyable, the real joys that last forever are our steadfast trust and joy in the Lord. Through good times and bad times, through sick times and healthy times, through the up times and down times, we need to express joy—because God has saved us from our sins.

When I embraced this concept, I was able to give my own disease and suffering to God and move on. I knew that I was in good medical and spiritual hands and that God wanted the best for me.

For Me to Live Is Christ

For me, to live is Christ

and to die is gain.

PHILIPPIANS 1:21 NIV

33

When I've felt that I'm not close to God, I realize that I'm the one who has moved away, not God. We can always step back into His presence by coming before Him, calling upon Him, and expressing our thanks to Him for all He has done for us.

The Lord is always there for you, waiting to fill your life with encouragement and affirmation, waiting mercifully to restore your soul. He does it through the words of Scripture, through the soft whisper of His Holy Spirit, and especially through the people who love, accept, and support you. God has little helpers everywhere who perform acts of encouragement for your hurting soul. Learn to appreciate all that they do to encourage you each day.

He Is Not Far Away

His purpose in all of this is that they should seek after God, and perhaps feel their way toward him and find him—though he is not far from any one of us.

ACTS 17:27

Father God, I really need to know that You are close by.

Your assurances mean a lot to me at this time.

You are truly my strength during these difficult days. Amen.

God Has a Plan

It is God himself who has made us what we are and given us new lives from Christ Jesus; and long ages ago he planned that we should spend these lives in helping others.

Ephesians 2:10

Isn't it good to know we are His workmanship, planned long ago? We are His ongoing project that hopefully glorifies Him. What a comfort it is to know that we are just where God has planned for us to be. You might be asking, "Does God really want me to be under this burden?" I'm here to tell you it's amazing to see how God can use *any* situation, if we keep open to His leading.

While Bob and I were in Seattle where I was undergoing cancer treatment, I can remember very vividly several couples who mentioned, "I'm so glad you are here so you can offer me comfort." Bob and I would look at each other with a nonverbal glance that said, "If our disease was for that one person, it was worth it." We knew God had a plan.

Sooner or later, all of us will go through deep troubles. When we are young or when life is treating us well, it's hard to think about the woes of life. They might happen to others, we think, but surely not to us or our family. But if the Lord grants an abundance of years, as He has in my life, we will all experience the woes I'm in the midst of:

› passing through deep waters
› wading through rivers
› walking through fire

But it is during this time I find that:

› God is with me.
› The rivers aren't sweeping over me.
› The fires aren't burning me.
› God is calling me by name, and I will fear no evil.

Fear Not

I have called you by name; you are mine. When you go through deep waters and great trouble, I will be with you. When you go through rivers of difficulty, you will not drown! When you walk through the fire of oppression, you will not be burned up—the flames will not consume you. For I am the Lord your God...

ISAIAH 43:1-3

If It's God's Will

I've had to change so many plans and priorities because of my illness or because God simply intervenes and rearranges everything. That doesn't mean I've become negative or that I've lost hope along the way. It means I've begun to realize that God has a master plan behind all of His mysteries. Only God knows what the future holds.

Lately, I have been studying the Lord's Prayer (Matthew 6:9-13 KJV), "Our Father which art in heaven, Hallowed be Thy name. Thy Kingdom come, Thy will be done." After all these years, I am still learning to accept and praise God for letting "Thy will be done" in my life.

What you ought to say is, "If the Lord wants us to, we shall live and do this or that."

JAMES 4:15

38

My grandson, Chad, is 20 years old. Over the years his biggest enemy has been his poor attitude. For his birthday a few years ago, Bob and I gave him a mug with the word "attitude" printed in large letters. He placed it on a shelf in his bedroom as a reminder, so when he wakes each morning he spots this mug and remembers that he can choose the proper attitude.

Choosing Your Attitude

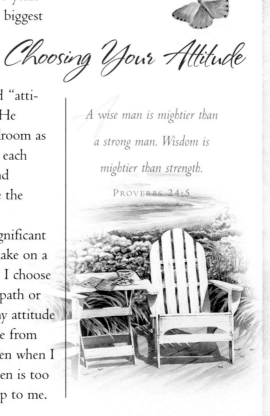

A wise man is mightier than a strong man. Wisdom is mightier than strength.

PROVERBS 24:5

This is the single most significant decision that you and I can make on a day-to-day basis. The attitude I choose either keeps me on a positive path or hinders my progress. When my attitude is proper, nothing can stop me from accomplishing my dreams. Even when I am in a deep valley—no burden is too great for me. My attitude is up to me.

He Guides All the Way

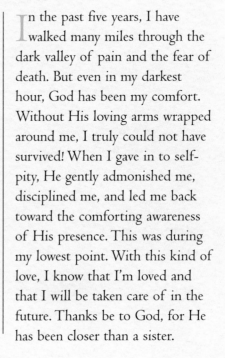

Even when walking through the dark valley of death I will not be afraid, for you are close beside me, guarding, guiding all the way.

PSALM 23:4

In the past five years, I have walked many miles through the dark valley of pain and the fear of death. But even in my darkest hour, God has been my comfort. Without His loving arms wrapped around me, I truly could not have survived! When I gave in to self-pity, He gently admonished me, disciplined me, and led me back toward the comforting awareness of His presence. This was during my lowest point. With this kind of love, I know that I'm loved and that I will be taken care of in the future. Thanks be to God, for He has been closer than a sister.

When the Lord has been gracious to our prayers, we should praise Him! Don't be silent; those around you need to hear of God's grace to you. As I have had so many of my prayers answered, I want to be the first to thank God in public for all He's done. My favorite Scripture during this dark period of my life has been John 11:4, which reads, "The purpose of his illness is not death, but for the glory of God. I, the Son of God, will receive glory from this situation."

Giving praise is the most heavenly of our Christian duties.

Let Others Know

And David danced before the Lord with all his might.

2 SAMUEL 6:14

When You Don't Know What to Pray

My heart says of you, "Seek his face!" Your face, LORD, I will seek.

PSALM 27:8 NIV

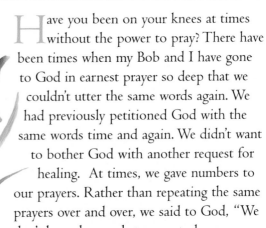

Have you been on your knees at times without the power to pray? There have been times when my Bob and I have gone to God in earnest prayer so deep that we couldn't utter the same words again. We had previously petitioned God with the same words time and again. We didn't want to bother God with another request for healing. At times, we gave numbers to our prayers. Rather than repeating the same prayers over and over, we said to God, "We don't have the words to pray today; so we ask that You hear prayer 14." Because we abide in Him and His words abide in us, He does hear our prayers—even when we don't know what to say.

Father God, let me be still and wait upon Your timing for all my prayers. I know You have heard them because You say You have. Slow me down, and let my heart's desires be Your will in my life. Amen.

Praise Him to Everyone

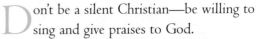

I will give repeated

thanks to the Lord,

praising him to everyone.

PSALM 109:30

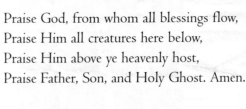

Don't be a silent Christian—be willing to sing and give praises to God.

The great doxology of the church, written by Thomas Ken and attributed to Louis Bourgeois, a German Psalter, took these words—

> Praise God, from whom all blessings flow,
> Praise Him all creatures here below,
> Praise Him above ye heavenly host,
> Praise Father, Son, and Holy Ghost. Amen.

—and made them ring out each Sunday in many of our churches. These words recognize that we are to praise our magnificent God. We are to be in a state of continuous praise for what He has done in our lives. He is everything to us: our Healer, our Provider, our Comforter, our Savior, our Redeemer, our Security.

Do you ever think about what God's morning message to us might be? Regardless of what the weather might be like, the message is always the same. He promises that the dawn will come at the beginning of each day. In all our troubles, He promises to be with us and to lift our burdens.

He wants to tell us that He will be alongside to help us through the day. He hasn't forgotten us. He understands our circumstances. He hears every prayer. The dawn brings a new day that contains the same promises of yesterday. Even during the darkness of night, God is there. You can trust His presence. He never leaves or forsakes us. Each new day has its dawn.

Always the Dawn

He lifts the burdens from those bent down beneath their loads. For the Lord loves good men.

PSALM 146:8

Give Them Away

May you be given more and more of God's kindness, peace, and love.

JUDE 2

When we are given "more and more" of something, we are given an abundance. The abundance that God has promised us is better than any worldly abundance we may want. He's promised us an abundance of the big three: kindness, peace, and love! If we're living in Him and obeying Him, our lives will overflow with these life-giving qualities.

God gives us what He promises, but we need to live His way. And in order to continue having these qualities in abundance, we must first give them away to others. It's the way God does things: The more we give, the more we get.

Do you ever have trouble sleeping? Then claim this promise. I know there can be plenty of nights that you might toss and turn. You just can't relax from thinking about your troubles or your sorrows. However, this verse tells me that I can lie down without fear and even have pleasant dreams.

Just remember that God knows all about your tomorrows. He's gone ahead of you to smooth out the rough patches. If He takes care of you today, He will certainly take care of you tomorrow. Lay your head on the pillow and know He will protect you from all harm.

Have Pleasant Dreams

When you lie down, you will not be afraid; when you lie down, your sleep will be sweet.

PROVERBS 3:24

Horatio G. Spafford wrote a beautiful song to console himself after losing his four daughters when their ship sank as they were traveling to Europe. Upon crossing the approximate spot of the ocean where the ship went down, he wrote the beautiful words to the Christian classic, "It Is Well with My Soul." Oh, if we could all sing such praises to God after a tragedy. He told God that no matter what, his soul trusted in the God who loved him. Here was a man who was able to see the big picture of life. He had a confidence far beyond most of our comprehension. He is a model for all of us.

It Is Well with My Soul

Day by day the Lord also pours out his steadfast love upon me, and through the night I sing his songs and pray to God who gives me life.

PSALM 42:8

48

Approaching the Throne of Grace

Let us come boldly to the very throne of God and stay there to receive his mercy

and to find grace to help us in our times of need.

True prayer is the drawing of my soul, by the grace of God, to the throne of God. It isn't just the speaking of words or the emotions of my petitions that matter. He cares that I approach Him in day-to-day conversation. My style isn't as important as my desire to be in communion with Him. There were times during my illness that my Bob and I felt our utterances weren't going beyond the ceiling; however, from the promises of Scripture on prayer, and from God's answers of past prayers, we knelt assured that they had reached His ears. Yes, we are to come with confidence to the throne of grace—where we obtain mercy and grace to help us in time of need.

Never Stop Praying

Always keep on praying.

1 Thessalonians 5:17

Throughout Scripture we are urged to "call upon the Lord" when we are sick, unable to provide for our families, or when our griefs overwhelm us. We are told to pray without ceasing for we have plenty of reasons to continually be in the Spirit.

Ever since my early Christian experience I have heard about prayer, but to be honest with you, I never really understood it. I knew I was to pray, but I wasn't sure how it worked in one's life. I have since realized that I never need to ask, "May I be permitted to come into Your presence?" God desires communication. To experience the abundance of God we only need to ask. Your Father in heaven is waiting to give you good gifts.

50

Words, words, words! Sometimes that's what the Bible seems to me. Sometimes—especially when life is going well—I read through whole passages without any sense of what the words really mean. But during the tough times, I find that the words of Scripture really come to life. The Word suddenly takes on a new depth of meaning.

The familiar words of Romans 8 are a wonderful comfort. They remind me that the Lord is with me in my pain, but He also is greater than my current suffering. I have often needed that assurance when I've been unsure of my own strength. Nothing can separate me from God's love—and that's more than just words! That's rock-solid, dependable, life-giving truth.

More than Words

For I am convinced that nothing can ever separate us from his love. Death can't, and life can't. The angels won't, and all the powers of hell itself cannot keep God's love away.

ROMANS 8:38

51

When Words Won't Come

For we don't even know what we should pray for nor how to pray as we should, but the Holy Spirit prays for us with such feeling that it cannot be expressed in words.

ROMANS 8:26

If I don't have the strength to utter words to heaven with my desires, God's grace will hear my desires without me speaking the words. The Holy Spirit speaks for us. God understands even those things that cannot be expressed in words. Parents often know what's in their children's minds without them even talking. Likewise a spouse instantaneously knows what the other is thinking. God is like this with us.

Don't be fearful to pray when you feel as if you don't have the words or energy. The Holy Spirit will renew your desire for prayer, and He will give you words to speak.

I so look forward to getting past the winter rains of life. I live for the day when I can return to a normal lifestyle—enjoying church, sporting events, and restaurants; eating a green salad, playing with a gathering of small children.

I have come to realize there are various seasons of one's life, and I can assure you that these last few months have not been easy on me or my family and friends. Everyone has been wonderful during this season of life. They have come alongside, assuring me that spring will come and I will join in the celebration. Come on, spring! I can't wait for you to arrive!

Spring Is Here

For the winter is past, the rain is over and gone. The flowers are springing up and the time of the singing of birds has come. Yes, spring is here.

SONG OF SOLOMON 2:11-12

Day by Day

Your heavenly Father knows your

needs. He will always give you all

you need from day to day.

LUKE 12:30-31

As of today, I've lived through 23,399 days, and I've found this promise in Luke to be true in my life everyday. I've had my ups and downs, but God has always provided for my needs. As a little girl with an alcoholic, sometimes violent father, I was protected. As a teenager living with my single-parent mom in the little apartment behind our dress store, I never went hungry or unclothed. As newlyweds in a tiny apartment, Bob and I often struggled to make ends meet, but there was always enough from day to day. Now, during my adult years, the Lord has graciously blessed me beyond all my expectations—materially and spiritually. God is truly the provider of all good things.

When the waves of life threaten to engulf us, we can keep our eyes on Him and face the storm with complete trust. "I will trust and not be afraid" (Isaiah 12:2). Each of us has storms sweep across our horizons. We can be overcome by fear and doubt and begin to sink, or we can be filled with faith and trust and walk triumphantly on the stormy waves. We have the option to put our trust completely in God and His promises. Fear and trust don't mix, just like oil and water. If trust is the oil, it will rise to the top; if fear is the oil, then it will rise to the top. Which one is your oil?

Fear or Trust?

Jesus immediately spoke to them, reassuring them. "Don't be afraid!" he said.

MATTHEW 14:27

No More Tears

He will wipe away all tears from
their eyes, and there shall be no more
death, nor sorrow, nor crying, nor
pain. All of that has gone forever.

REVELATION 21:4

Who else can give us a promise like this one? It's an exciting glimpse of what life in eternity with Him will be like. Just think of life with no more tears, no more death, no more sorrow, no more crying! These will all disappear forever. Hard to imagine, isn't it? We live in a fallen and depraved world; as a result, our lives are often dysfunctional. But those who have followed Christ won't live like that forever—we have God's promise on that. Someday all our pain will be wiped away, never to be experienced again. I look forward with great anticipation to that heavenly event. I hope you are there with me.

Throughout Scripture, we read of victory over troubles and suffering. Philosopher Peter Wust said, "The great things happen to those who pray. But we learn to pray best in suffering."

Prayer, suffering, joy, and the surprises of God...they are all tightly enmeshed. But many people shrink from suffering, afraid that it will kill their joy and keep them from experiencing "great things." When we are rightly related to God, life is full of joyful uncertainty and expectancy. We do not know what God is going to do next; He packs our lives with surprises all the time. Prayer becomes the lens through which we begin to see from God's perspective.

So Let It Grow

Is your life full of difficulties and temptations? Then be happy, for when the way is rough, your patience has a chance to grow.

JAMES 1:2-3

57

Father God, I've called out to You for healing, and I've been disappointed when You haven't done what I've expected. Let me be patient with Your calendar. I know you don't set Your clock by my watch. Even to the end, I believe You have planned my coming in and my going out. Amen.

We must remember that our prayers are to be offered in submission to God's will for our lives. Just because God hears our prayers doesn't mean He always gives us everything we ask for. However, He does give us everything that is good for us. Knowing God's will for our lives is impossible unless we get to know the character of God. We know Him by being with Him in study and prayer. Only then can our prayers be like gold. Gold is purified by extreme heat that burns out all the impurities of the ore. Sometimes when we pray, God is replying, "Not yet." God's timing is always perfect— never too soon and never too late. Trust Him!

All That We Need

I am with you; that is all that you need. My power shows up best in weak people.

2 Corinthians 12:9

God Is Great

O Lord God! You have made the

heavens and earth by your great

power; nothing is too hard for you!

JEREMIAH 32:17

I don't know why I even try to understand God with my tiny brain. He is so much greater than I am. I stand in awe when I journey to the mountains, the desert, or the beach, and see all of His creations. He truly is awesome, and I know He can do anything!

But even though I can't always understand Him, I do trust Him to do what He has promised. I pray that God's will might be done in my life and that I will be able to hear and accept His direction.

W e make a big mistake if we forget to calm our spirits and seek the stillness that we need to walk peacefully in this crazy world. The psalmist urged, "Be still, and know that I am God." Easier said than done, right? Let me urge you today in the strongest possible terms: Do whatever it takes to nurture stillness in your life. Don't let the enemy wear you so thin that you lose your balance and perspective. Regular time for stillness is as important and necessary as sleep, exercise, and nutritious food. Be available to God, to yourself, and then, ultimately, to others.

Be Still My Soul

Wear my yoke—for it fits

perfectly—and let me teach you;

for I am gentle and humble, and

you shall find rest for your souls;

for I give you only light burdens.

MATTHEW 11:29

Learning Lesson

Since the Lord is directing

our steps, why try to

understand everything that

happens along the way?

PROVERBS 20:24

*B*ut God, are You sure that You meant this *trial for me? Didn't You mean for it to go to someone else? I'm sure You made a mistake when You gave me this burden.* Does that kind of thinking sound familiar? I know it crossed my mind once or twice. However, after I got over the shock and my emotions came back to earth, I knew I had two choices: be angry at God, or accept what I was about to go through and realize that this situation was going to make me a better person. Trials are never wasted, nor does God give them to the wrong person. Through all the pain, tears, hurts, inconveniences, and prayers, we learn to grow and depend on His Word.

One Day at a Time

You saw me before I was born and scheduled each day of my life before I began to breathe.

Every day was recorded in your book!

PSALM 139:16

God, who loves us, numbers our days—but we don't know how many we will have. God, who loves us, will direct our paths—but we don't know where they will take us or what we will discover along the way. God has given you the gift of this moment, this day—it's full of blessings and opportunities. Gifts are made to be used, not just stored on a shelf. So tear off the wrapping, pull apart the tissue paper, and say yes to whatever you find.

Most of all, say yes to the Lord, who loves you. Give Him back the gift of your hours and your days.

Oh God, as You stand in heaven, I beg You to be stirred about my situation. React to my pleading and don't desert me now! I need You today more than any other time in my life. My sufferings tremble when You come to my defense. I put myself and my problem into Your loving, all-knowing, all-wise care. Amen.